Not For You

Volume I

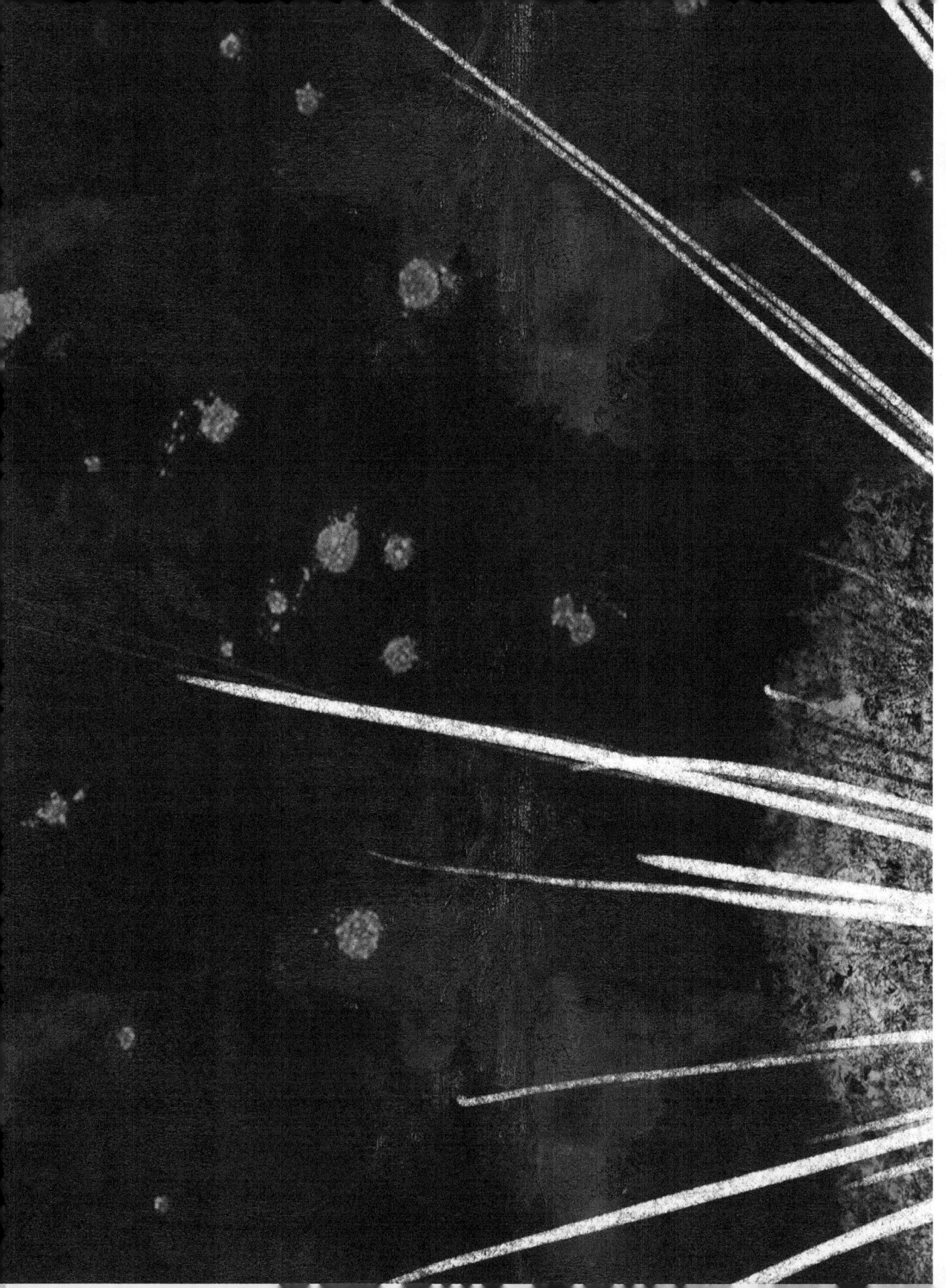

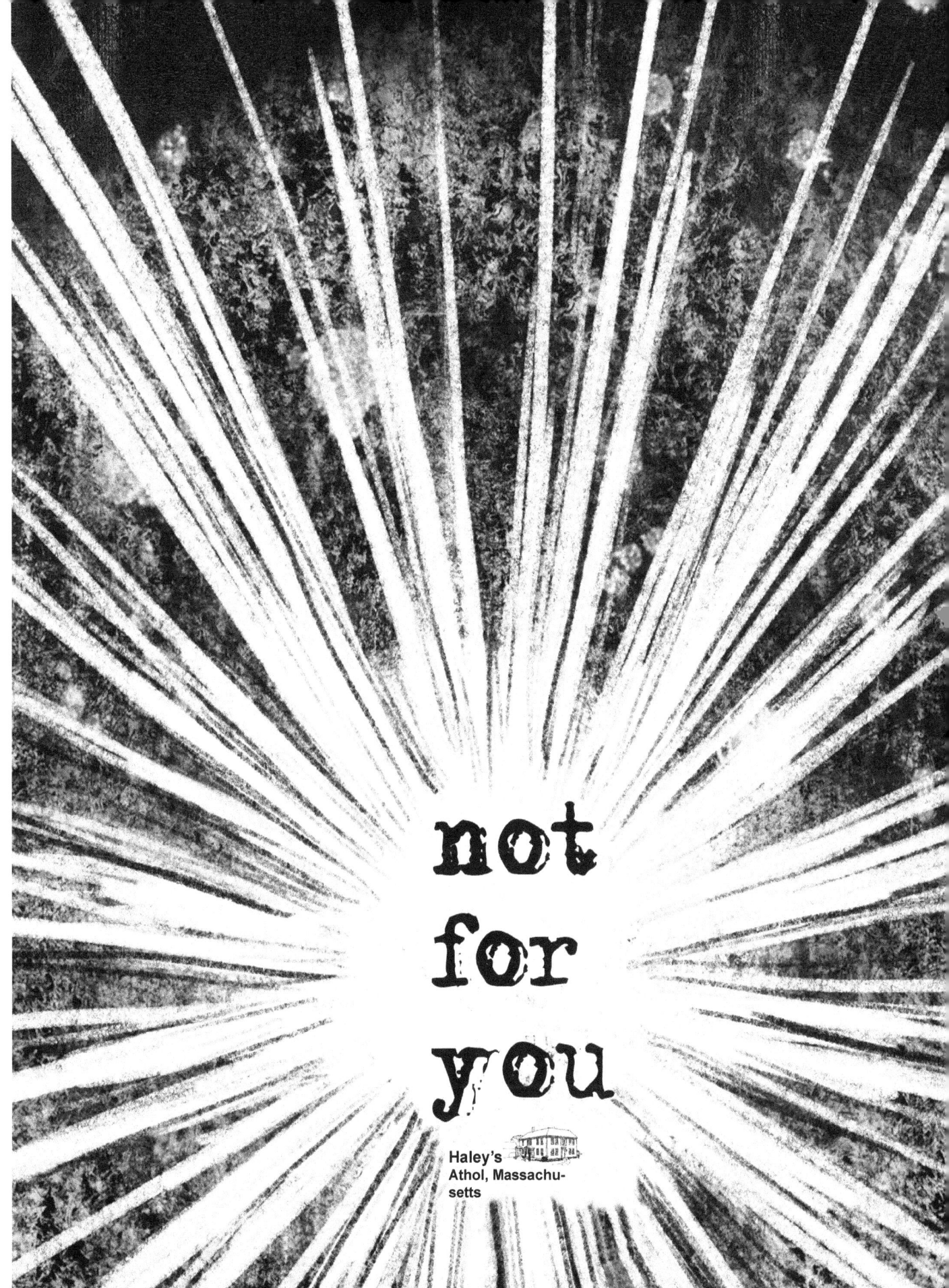

not

for

you

Haley's
Athol, Massachu-
setts

Haley's
488 South Main Street
Athol, MA 01331
800.215.8805

International Standard Book Number, hardcover: 978-1-956055-01-6
International Standard Book Number, eBook pdf: 978-1-956055-02-3
Library of Congress Control Number: 2023949897

For Gabe

Thanks to everyone that has been so supportive.
Special thanks to the studio: Red House Irons
& my parents.
Without the studio and them, none of this would
be   possible.

The Moon seems to glow in the night sky,

softly illuminating the sleepy world below.

We only have one special moon
    created from chunks of the earth in the

    early development of the solar system

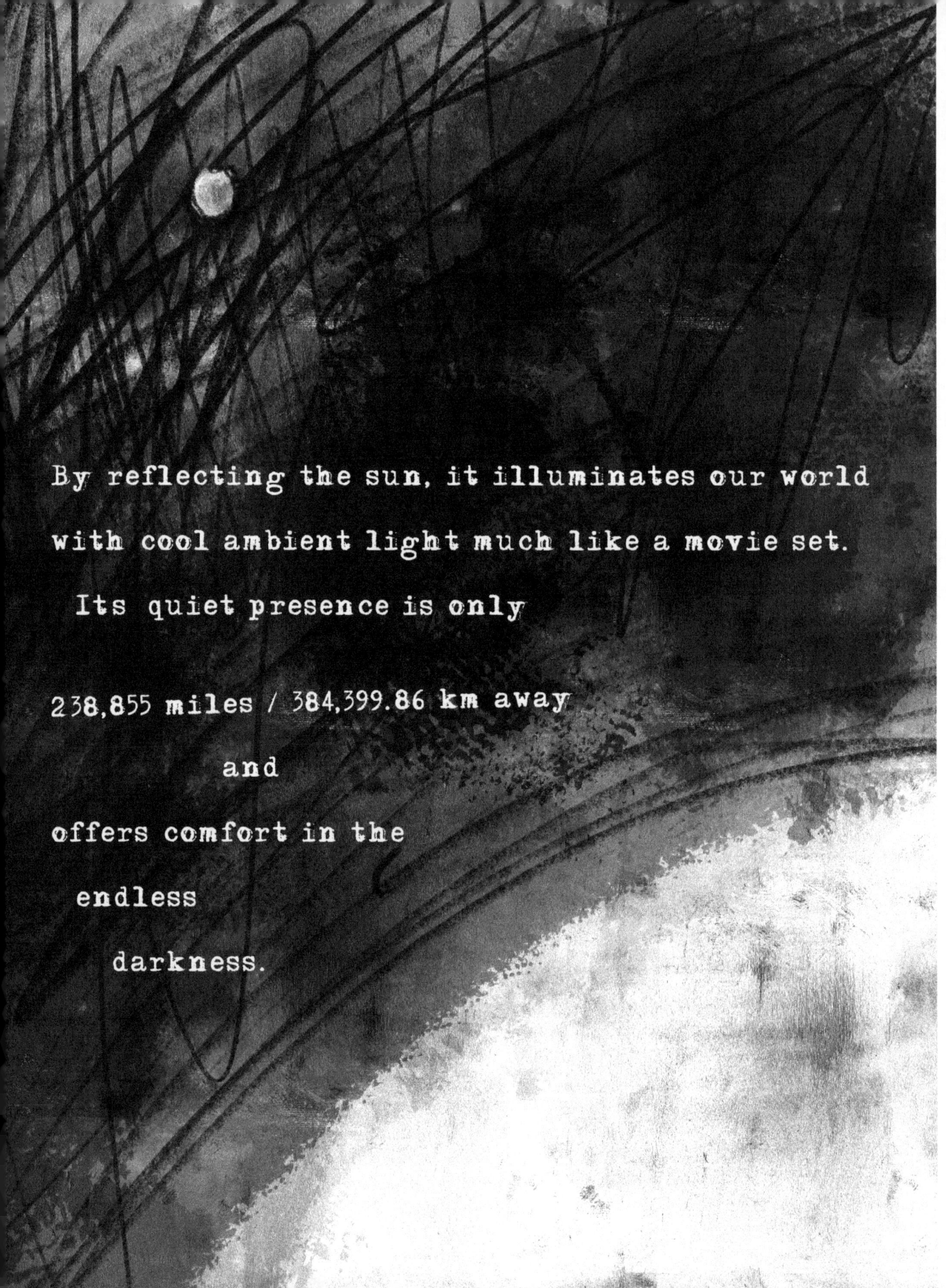

By reflecting the sun, it illuminates our world with cool ambient light much like a movie set. Its quiet presence is only

238,855 miles / 384,399.86 km away

and

offers comfort in the

endless

darkness.

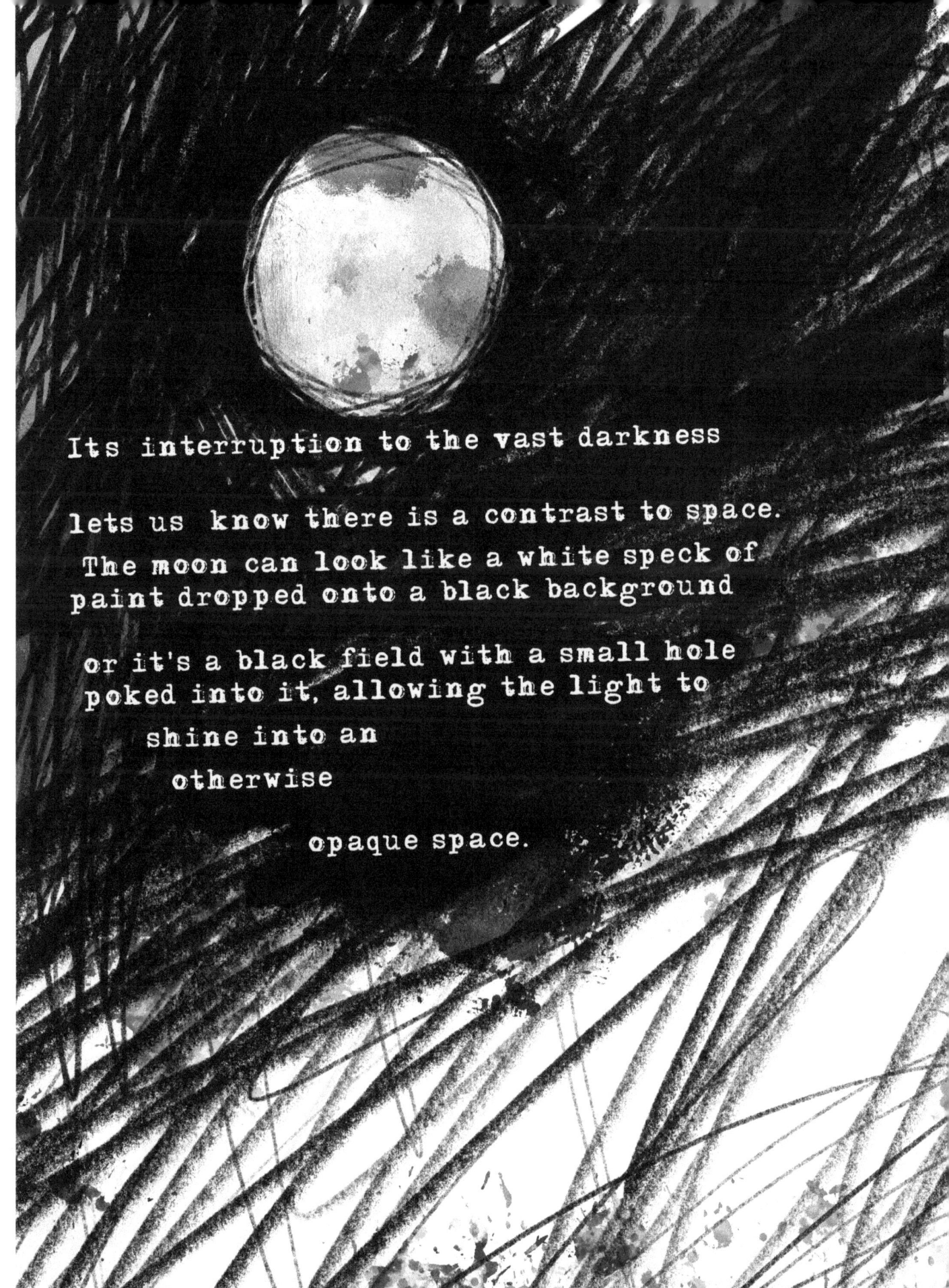

Its interruption to the vast darkness

lets us know there is a contrast to space.
The moon can look like a white speck of
paint dropped onto a black background

or it's a black field with a small hole
poked into it, allowing the light to

shine into an

otherwise

opaque space.

Regardless of the perspective,

the moon does not reflect its  cool light


for you my love.

It is just the remains from a

cosmic impact.

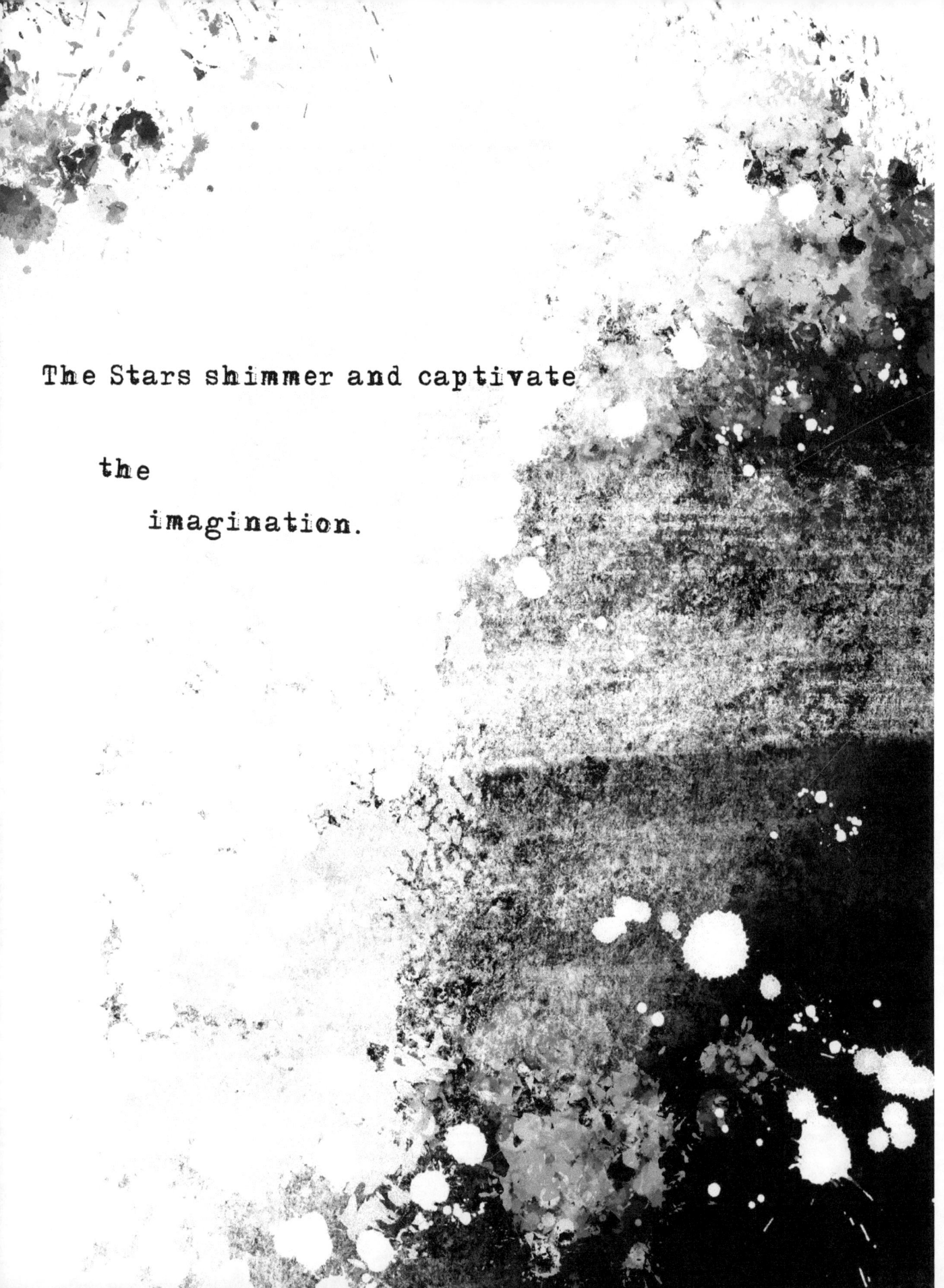

The Stars shimmer and captivate

the

imagination.

They sparkle, twinkle, and dance in
    the night sky.

                    Not unlike the moon,

            they give contrast

to
        the endless darkness of the universe.


They are worlds, planets, suns, and moons

    for about
                seven trillion light-years across.

The light that twinkles

   and
dances for those moments can be wished upon


   – the origin of that sparkle might

   already be long extinct.

That means some of the dancing stars we see

no longer exist

and

we are witnessing just an echo
of what once was...

it's the past.

The

Sun shines sO

brightly

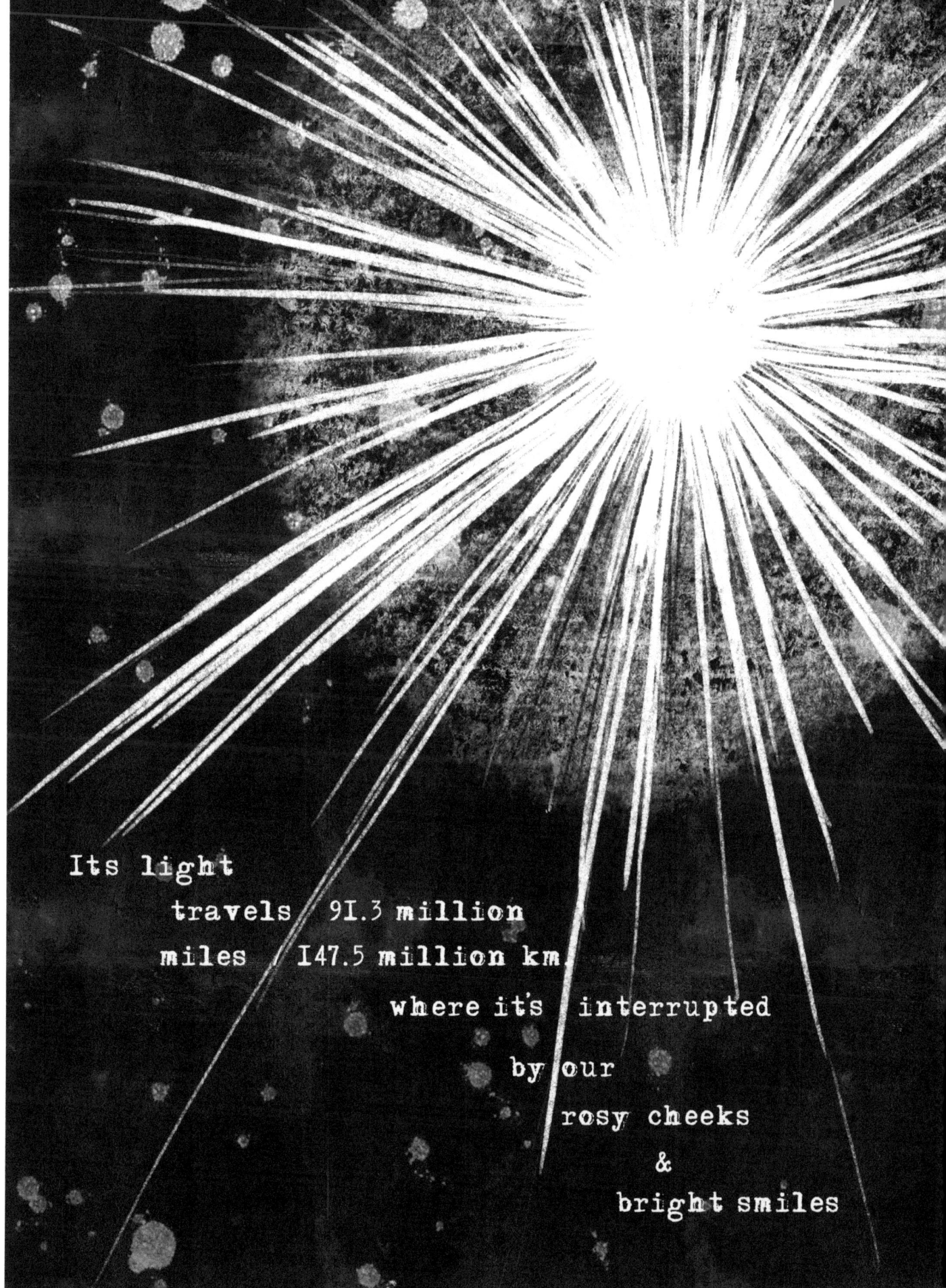

Its light
    travels   91.3 million
    miles  / 147.5 million km
        where it's / interrupted

           by our

           rosy cheeks
              &
           bright smiles

What we experience
of
its
comfort is energy
that starts as a disturbance
in an

electromagnetic
fiel<sub>d</sub>

The sun sends out lots

and lots of radiation

that passes through the solar system

&

continues
beyond our

disrupted

smiles.

Its light gives plants and animals

life

&       shines so beautifully...

. . .but it's not for you, my love.

You are

just another object

in
the

way

You are composed of & influenced by all these incredible things.

You are only a very – very – very – very small interruption to all these things.

None of this is here for you,

the moon, stars, or sun.

Life is the exception to the rule.

Time extends beyond our ability
to understand,

& one day

these experiences

will no longer inspire you,

kiss your cheeks with warmth,

or light up your

night
sky.

Because it's not for you.

You are just here now to witness it.

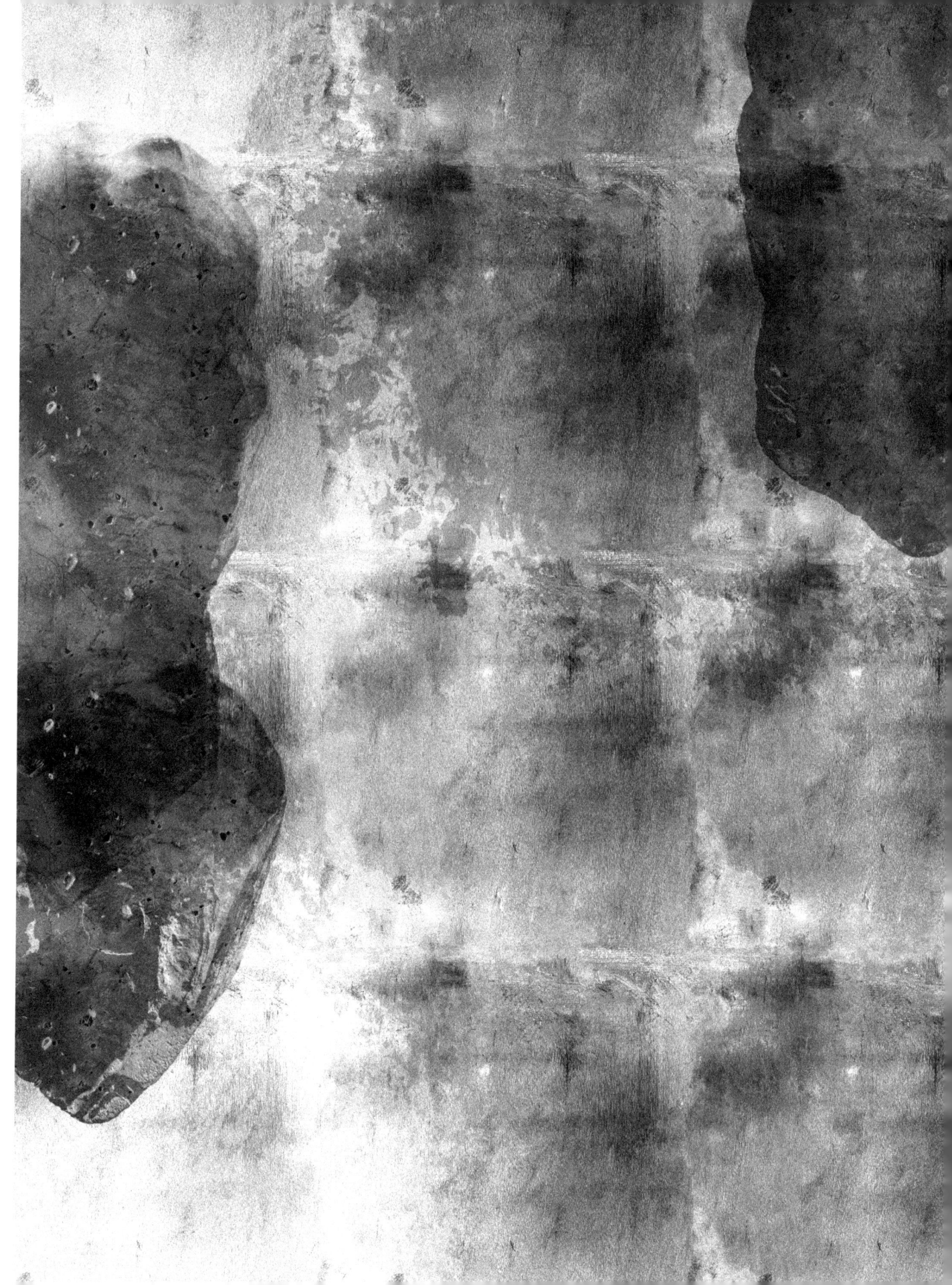

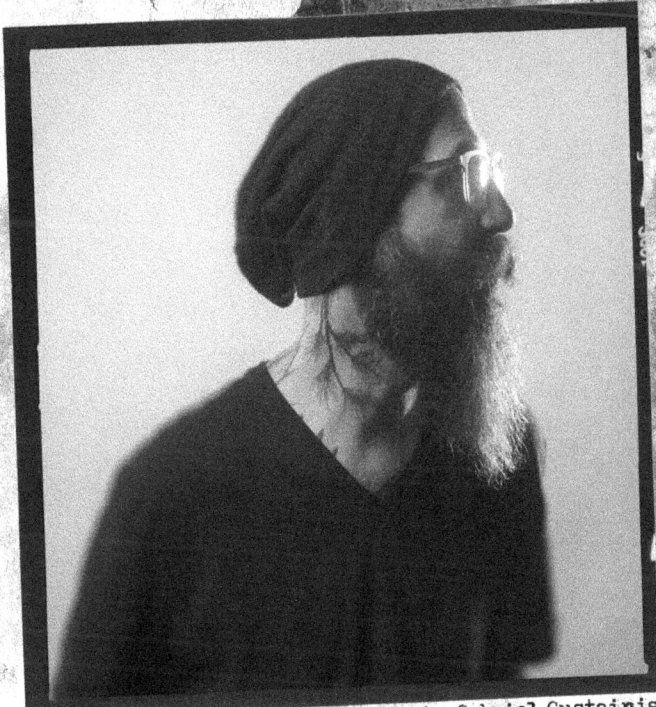

photo: Gabriel Gustainis

about:

Thomas's work is influenced by the philosophic values of traditional folk art: it s social function, utilitarianism, empowerment, and the ability to reflect aspects of the individual.

Thomas's work has been developed by his graduate studies (MFA from TUFTS Univ.) as well as what he has learned from working with amazing people over the years. His work continues to grow and merge into new mediums.

His work as a tattoo artist, photographer,& illustrator supports his visual lexicon along with exploring the mountains looking to further refine his craft through new opportunities & experiences.